EXPLORING THE SUN

By Emily Kington

CONTENTS

MIX
Paper | Supporting responsible forestry
FSC® C158492

First published in 2026 by Hungry Tomato Ltd
F15, Old Bakery Studios, Blewetts Wharf, Malpas Road,
Truro, Cornwall, TR1 1QH, UK.

A CIP catalogue record for this book is available from the British Library.

ISBN 9781835697061

Printed in China

Discover more at
www.hungrytomato.com

Front cover image is an edited image of the Sun.
Title page image is an edited image of the Sun.
Contents page image is an edited image of the Sun.

Words in **BOLD** can be found in the glossary.

WHERE IS THE SUN?

The Sun is the centre of our **solar system**! Without it, our solar system would not exist.

All the planets, **moons,** and **asteroids** in the solar system **orbit** around the Sun. The Sun is a **star**. A star creates light and heat.

It's the closest star to Earth. When you look in the night sky you can see thousands of stars, but they are all much further away than the Sun is.

SUN FACTS

The Sun gives all the planets in our solar system heat and light. There wouldn't be any life on Earth without it.

The Sun is always shining. Even if it's nighttime where you live, the Sun is shining somewhere else!

It is over 150 million kilometres (93 million miles) away from Earth. That's close enough to keep us warm but also far enough away that it's not too hot!

The Sun is also huge – over a million Earths would fit inside it!

Sun

WHAT IS THE SUN MADE OF?

The Sun is made mostly of hot **gases** called **hydrogen** and **helium**.

Hydrogen makes up nearly three quarters of all of the Sun's gases. Almost a quarter of it is helium. There are also tiny amounts of **oxygen** and other **elements**.

These gases are constantly burning, producing the Sun's light and heat.

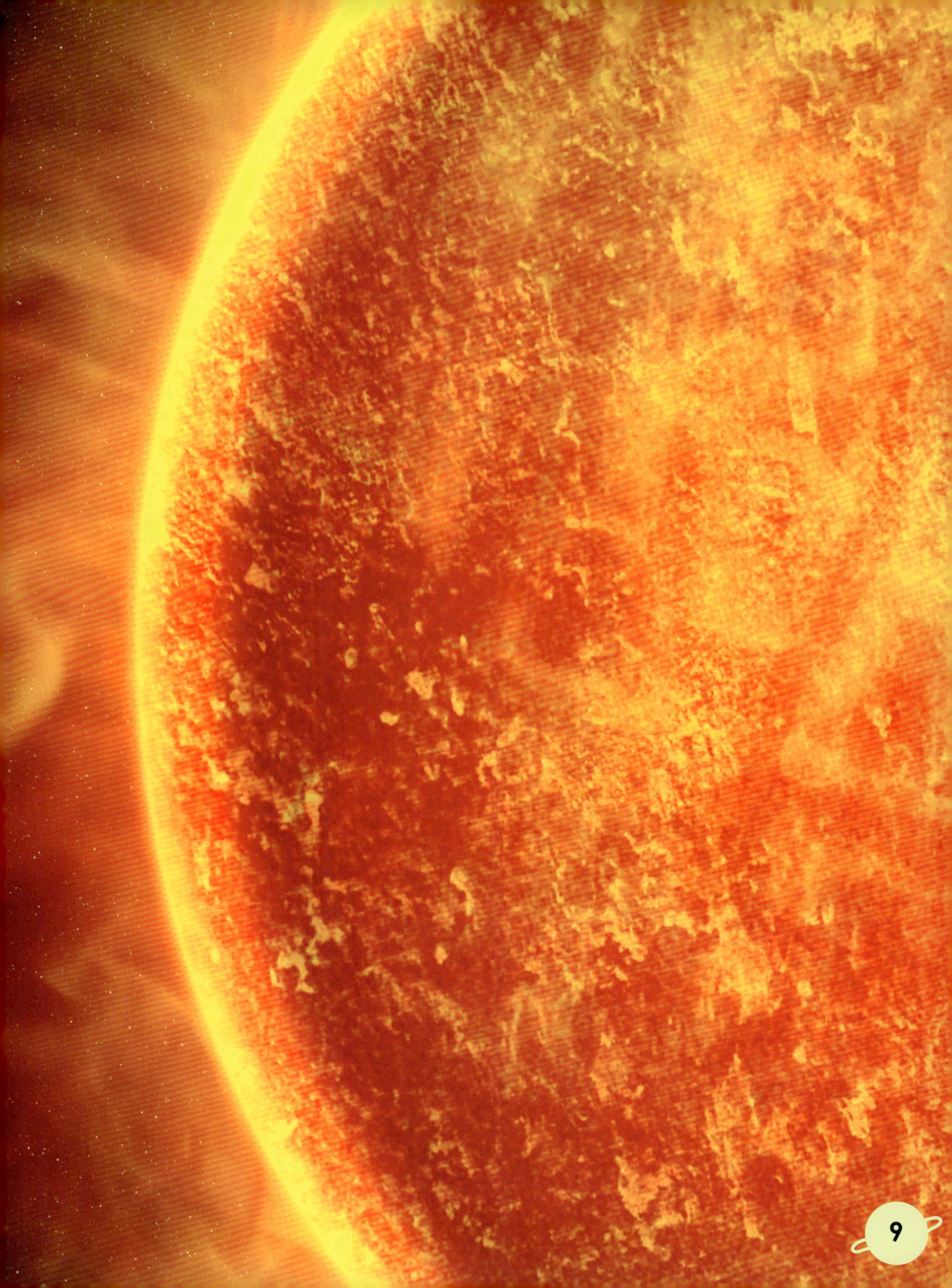

THE BIRTH OF THE SUN

The Sun began its life over four billion years ago as a huge cloud of spinning gas and dust.

It collapsed under the weight of its own **gravity**, flattening into a disc and spinning quicker and quicker.

Most of the gas and dust was pulled to the centre to form the Sun. The remaining material formed the planets and other natural **satellites** that now orbit the Sun.

The solar system

THE SUN'S LIFE

Everything has a lifespan – including the Sun. But don't worry, it has lots of time left.

The Sun creates heat by burning gases. It will eventually run out of this **fuel**, but not for another five billion years!

When it does run out of fuel, the Sun will grow bigger and bigger and turn into a **red giant**.

Its outer layers will then gradually disappear, leaving only its **core**. This will cool the Sun down and turn it into a **white dwarf**!

White dwarf

SUNSPOTS AND FLARES

You must never look directly at the Sun! Its light is extremely bright and can damage your eyes permanently. Scientists use special equipment to study the Sun.

They know that it's always changing. Two of its most amazing features are sunspots and solar flares.

Sunspots are dark areas on the Sun's surface. They may be cooler than other parts of the Sun, but they are still incredibly hot at 3,800 °C (6872 °F)!

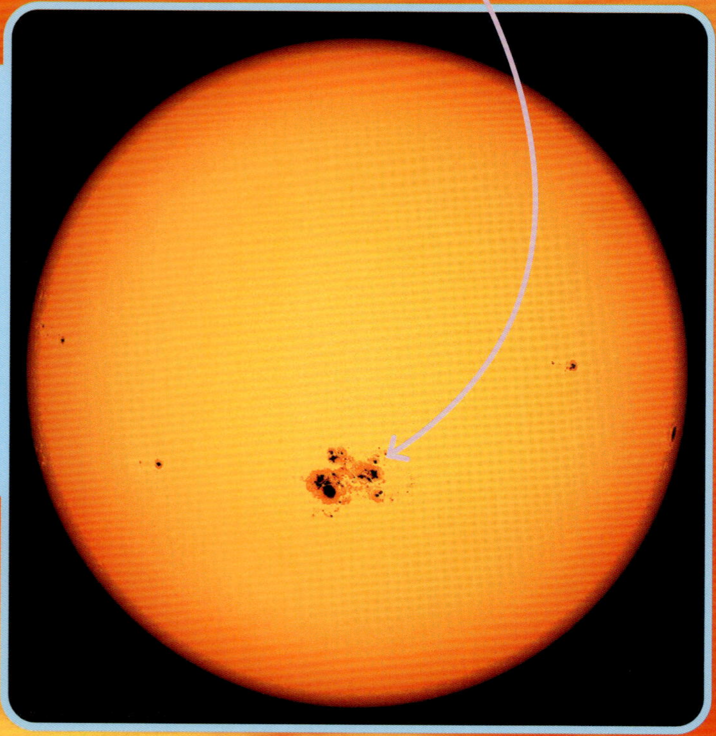

Solar flare

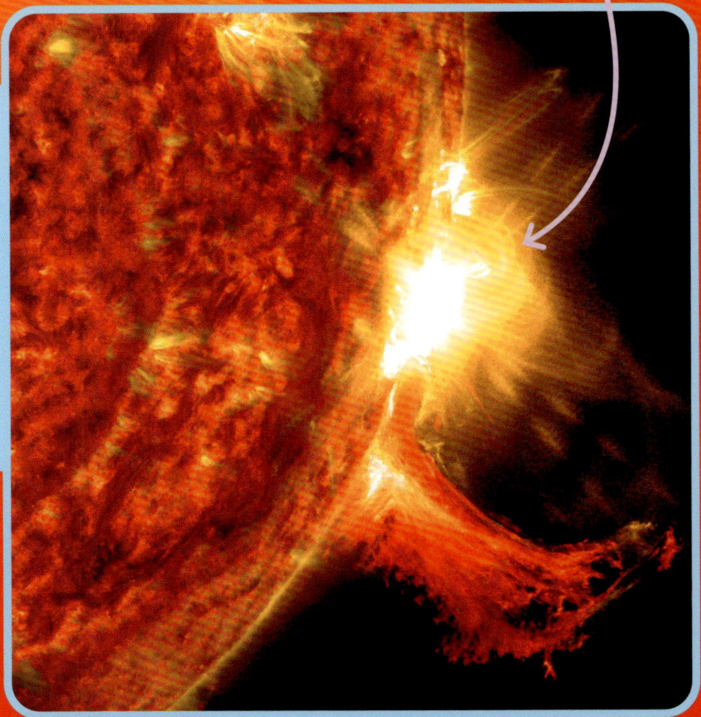

A solar flare is a huge explosion that sends waves of very hot **particles** out into space. Satellites watch out!

ECLIPSES

Sometimes the Moon moves between Earth and the Sun. When they line up in this special way, the Moon blocks the light from the Sun and causes an eclipse.

A total eclipse makes the sky dark even in the middle of the day.

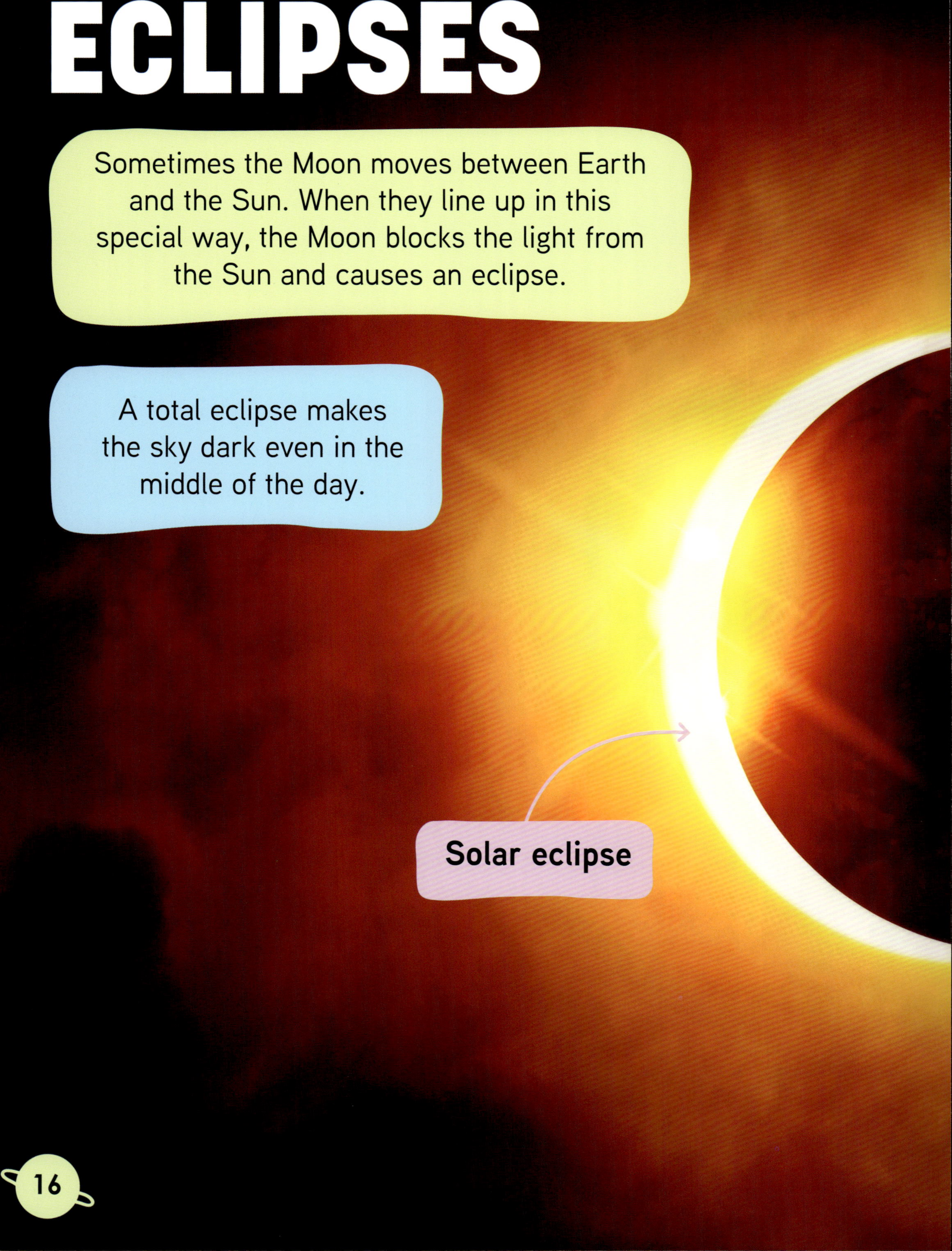

A partial eclipse means that only part of the Sun is covered by the Moon. The amount of darkness depends on how much of the Sun is blocked.

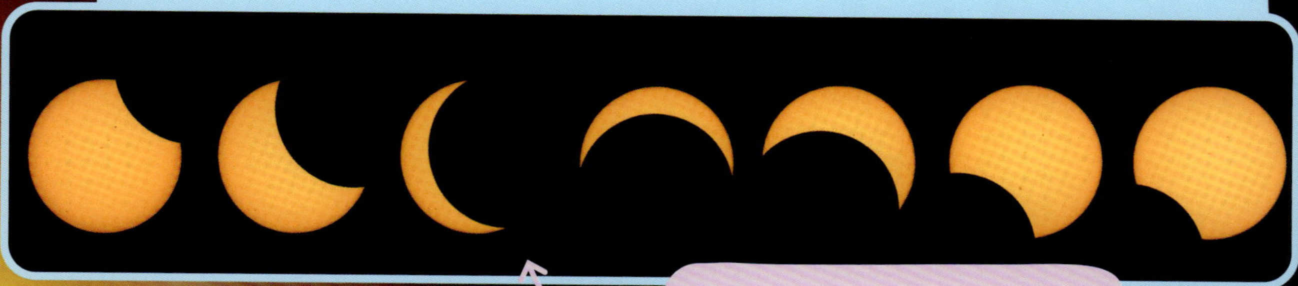

Partial eclipses

You can only see a solar eclipse from certain places on Earth and you must wear special protective glasses to see it.

EARTH'S PROTECTION

Although we need the Sun for heat and light, all kinds of rays come from the Sun that are dangerous to life on Earth.

Earth is surrounded by a layer of gases called the **atmosphere**. It's like a protective bubble. It holds the air that we breathe and it's where the weather happens.

It also blocks invisible rays from the Sun that are harmful to us. These are rays that can burn our skin and damage the **cells** in our bodies.

FACT FILE

Scientists studying the Sun learn lots of amazing facts about it. There is so much more still to learn, too!

A lunar eclipse happens when the Earth moves in front of the Sun and casts a shadow on the Moon. It can make the Moon appear to be red or orange. Scientists call this a 'blood moon'! It only happens when there is a **full moon**.

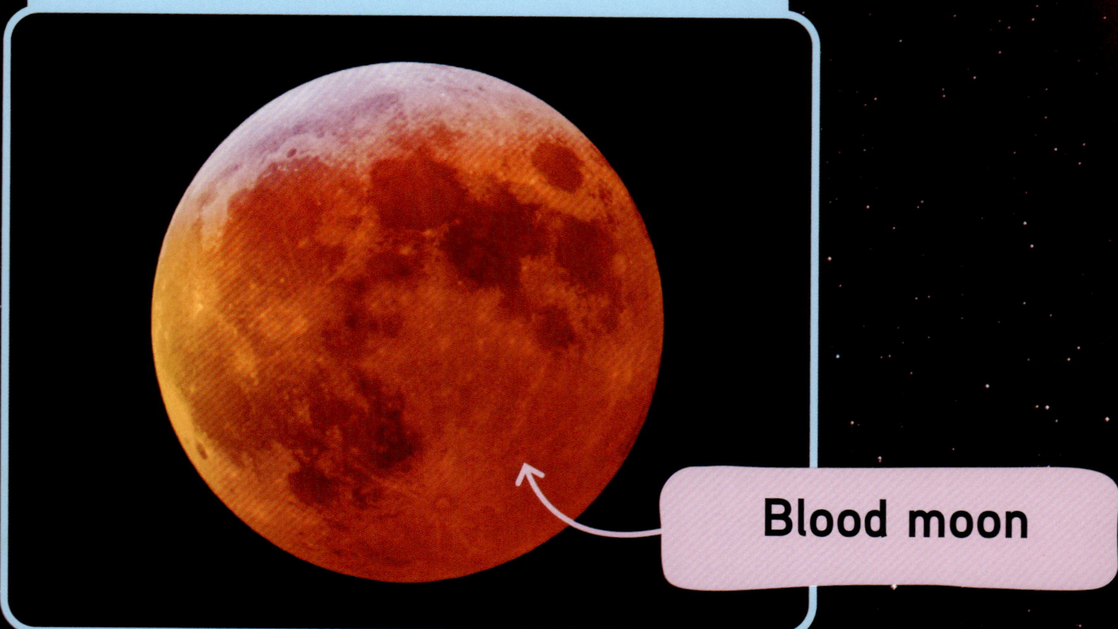

Solar wind blows out from the Sun in all directions and at very high speeds of over 1 million miles per hour (1.6 million kilometres per hour). It's like an invisible storm racing through space!

WHAT'S NEXT?

One of the problems of studying the Sun is the fact that it's so hot. Building spacecraft that can withstand such heat is a mission in itself!

Parker Solar Probe

NASA's Parker Solar Probe launched in 2018 to study the Sun's outer atmosphere.

Parker Solar Probe launch

It sped through space, flying 6.1 million kilometres (3.8 million miles) above the surface of the Sun. It was super speedy and reached an incredible 430,000 mph (692,000 kph), making it the fastest human-made object ever. And it survived!

GLOSSARY

Asteroids – small space rocks that orbit the Sun.

Atmosphere – the gases that surround a planet or star.

Cells – the smallest parts of a living thing.

Core – the middle of a planet or star.

Elements – substances that are the the building blocks of everything that exists.

Fuel – things that are burned to make energy.

Full Moon – a phase of the Moon where all of it is visible from Earth.

Gases – Substances that are neither solid nor liquid, and have no fixed shape. Many gases are invisible.

Gravity – an invisible force that pulls things together. Gravity keeps our feet on the ground and the planets spinning around the Sun.

Helium – a colourless, tasteless gas.

Hydrogen – a colourless, tasteless gas.

Moons – large, natural objects that orbit a planet.

Orbit – the path taken by one object circling around another in space.

Oxygen – an invisible gas in the air that people and animals need to breathe.

Particles – tiny pieces of something.

Satellites – things that orbit around a planet. They can be natural, like the Moon, or human-made.

Solar System – the Sun and everything that moves around it.

Star – a bright ball of gas in space that gives off light and heat.

Red giant – a very large star that has reached the end of its life and is cooling down.

White dwarf – the core of a star left over after the star has used up all of its energy.

Picture credits:
(t=top; b=bottom; m=middle; l=left; r=right):

NASA: images-assets.nasa.gov/image/GSFC_20171208_Archive_e000962/GSFC_20171208_Archive_e000962~orig.jpg 15br; images-assets.nasa.gov/image/NHQ201708210308/NHQ201708210308~orig.jpg 17t; images-assets.nasa.gov/image/NHQ201808120015/NHQ201808120015~orig.TIF 23tl; images-assets.nasa.gov/image/PIA07335/PIA07335~orig.jpg 10m; images-assets.nasa.gov/image/PIA11800/PIA11800~orig.jpg 11br; images-assets.nasa.gov/image/PIA11800/PIA11800~orig.jpg 14br. Shutterstock: 1bg; 1059 SHU 6bl; Abia adeel 6-7bg; Alones 7tr; Andrei Armiagov 2-3bg; Claudio Caridl 21tr; Muratart 18-19bg, 20-21bg, 22-23bg; Nazarii_Neshcherenskyi 12br; New Africa 14-15bg; Nixx Photography 8-9; Paul Shuang 24bg; Primoz Cigler 20bl; Triff 4-5bg, 10-11bg; Vadim sadovski 12-13bg; Vibe Images 16-17bg.